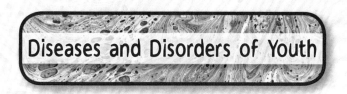

Diseases and Disorders of Youth

Kids and Mental Illness

Peggy J. Parks

ReferencePoint
Press®

San Diego, CA

© 2019 ReferencePoint Press, Inc.
Printed in the United States

For more information, contact:
ReferencePoint Press, Inc.
PO Box 27779
San Diego, CA 92198
www.ReferencePointPress.com

LIBRARY OF CONGRESS CATALOGING-IN-PUBLICATION DATA

Name: Parks, Peggy J., 1951– author.
Title: Kids and Mental Illness/by Peggy J. Parks.
Description: San Diego, CA: ReferencePoint Press, Inc., 2019. | Series:
    Diseases and Disorders of Youth | Audience: Grade 9 to 12. | Includes
    bibliographical references and index.
Identifiers: LCCN 2017054543 (print) | LCCN 2017056815 (ebook) | ISBN
    9781682824023 (eBook) | ISBN 9781682824016 (hardback)
Subjects: LCSH: Adolescent psychopathology—Juvenile literature. |
    Youth—Mental health—Juvenile literature.
Classification: LCC RJ503 (ebook) | LCC RJ503 .P364 2019 (print) | DDC
    616.8900835—dc23
LC record available at https://lccn.loc.gov/2017054543

Contents

Disorders of the Mind

Benjamin Shapiro was just eight years old when he began seeing a psychotherapist. His parents decided to take him for therapy because he had developed some peculiar rituals, and they were concerned about him. He felt the need, for instance, to touch certain objects a specific number of times or flip light switches on and off, also for a specific number of times. The boy had become convinced that by doing these rituals, he could control important events in his life, such as preventing his parents from dying and keeping the world safe for them and other people he loved. Shapiro explains his reasoning as a child: "If I touch my doorknob eight times, Mom and Dad will come home unharmed. If I read the same page six times in a row, I won't be orphaned."[1] He was diagnosed with obsessive-compulsive disorder, a mental illness most commonly known as OCD.

Like other OCD sufferers, Shapiro performed the rituals (known as compulsions) in a futile effort to calm his irrational fears (known as obsessions). He hated the rituals but did not dare stop performing them. "They had an irrational logic which made me feel protected and allowed me to function," he says. Those feelings of protection suddenly disappeared when Shapiro turned twelve years old. That year, he says, "something cracked." Rather than the rituals helping him function, his OCD began to control him, which was completely debilitating. "I had to be out of school for four months, spent my days with tutors and therapists, and had thoughts about dying,"[2] he says.

An Old Myth Dispelled

OCD is one of numerous mental illnesses that can affect children and teens. These disorders can differ significantly, based on characteristics, symptoms, age of onset, and level of impairment. Still, a basic definition applies to them all: Mental illnesses are conditions that affect brain function, which means they interfere with thinking, emotions, moods, and/or behavior.

Scientific examination of mental illness traces back centuries, but that research was limited to studying adults. The belief that children and adolescents also suffered from diseases of the mind did not become credible until the early to mid-twentieth century. Until then, the prevailing scientific belief was that youth could not develop mental illness because they were spared from the stress and anxiety faced by adults. Any emotional problems children exhibited were typically blamed on bad behavior. Such problems, according to the authors of a 2015 paper on the history of child psychiatry, "were largely considered moral problems, thus deserving punishment."[3]

During the mid-twentieth century, such rigid, simplistic views about mental illness in young people began to change. Study after study clearly showed that children and adolescents could—and did—suffer from many of the same mental illnesses as adults. The authors of the 2015 paper write: "The second half of the [twentieth] century, after World War II, witnessed an explosion in research with big advances in the understanding of the nature of childhood mental disorders, their diagnosis and classification."[4]

Up until the mid-twentieth century, mental illnesses in children were largely considered to be misbehaviors deserving of punishment. Today, experts know that young people can suffer from the same mental disorders as adults.

Growth of Scientific Knowledge

This research, which has been conducted over decades, has led to a vast store of scientific data related to youth mental illness. One of the primary research objectives has been, and continues to be, the human brain. The command and control center of the human body, the brain regulates everything from thinking, remembering, feeling, seeing, and hearing to the ability to walk, talk, and laugh. Scientists emphasize that the brain provides the key to fully understanding how mental illnesses develop—and because the brain is so complex, there are still far more questions than answers.

A particularly important finding in brain research is related to brain development. Scientists now know that the human brain develops from back to front and does not finish developing until people are in their mid- to late twenties. Because their brains are not fully developed, teens are more vulnerable than adults to addiction and some types of mental illness. The National Institute of Mental Health writes: "All the big changes the brain is experiencing may explain why adolescence is the time when many mental disorders—such as schizophrenia, anxiety, depression, bipolar disorder, and eating disorders—emerge."[5]

Along with profound discoveries about the brain, research has provided scientists with many other details about youth mental illness. One study from the early twenty-first century, for instance, revealed that anxiety had increased significantly among youth since the 1950s. Another showed that among people suffering from mental illness, about half developed their illness before they were fourteen years old. Also revealed through research was that mental illness can take many forms, ranging from fairly mild to so severe that the person may need to be cared for in a hospital. And despite the serious toll mental illness can take on young people, research has shown that only a fraction of children and adolescents with mental illness receive the treatment they need.

> "All the big changes the brain is experiencing may explain why adolescence is the time when many mental disorders—such as schizophrenia, anxiety, depression, bipolar disorder, and eating disorders—emerge."[5]
>
> —The National Institute of Mental Health, the United States' lead agency for research on mental disorders

A Widespread Problem

These and other studies have vastly broadened scientific understanding of youth mental illness. Despite this growth in knowledge, however, public awareness remains low. People often do not know, for instance, that at least half of all mental illness cases occur before age fourteen, and 75 percent occur by age twenty-four. It is also largely unknown that mental illnesses among children and teens are more common than chronic physical diseases such as asthma and diabetes. According to the National Alliance on Mental Illness (NAMI), one in every four to five youth aged thirteen to eighteen in the United States suffers from some type of mental illness. Many people are unaware of the symptoms of mental illness and how to tell the difference between normal teenage hormonal behavior and depression or severe anxiety. It is critical for parents, educators, counselors, clergy, and others who work with young people to understand what to look for.

"Mental illness is nothing to be ashamed of. It is a medical condition, just like heart disease or diabetes."[6]

—The American Psychiatric Association, the world's leading psychiatric organization

Scientists are aggressively pursuing research into child and adolescent mental illness, which will expand their knowledge even further. US health officials understand the urgency of increasing public awareness of this important topic and are committed to the task. They are also searching for ways to assure young people suffering from mental illness that they should not be embarrassed about reaching out for help. "Mental illness is nothing to be ashamed of," says the American Psychiatric Association. "It is a medical condition, just like heart disease or diabetes. And mental health conditions are treatable."[6]

Chapter 1

What Is Mental Illness?

As a psychiatrist, Rob Haskell works with patients who suffer from a variety of mental illnesses. The most prevalent of these among his teenage patients is anxiety disorders. "There is no mental illness I see more frequently in young people—because there is no mental illness more common in young people—than anxiety," says Haskell. One of his patients, a teenage boy whom he refers to as Joseph, was overwhelmed by anxiety. Desperate to escape from it, he rode his bike to a Pacific Ocean beach, entered the water, and started to swim. He kept swimming, Haskell explains, "following the sun as it dipped over the horizon, until the busy boardwalk sounds had faded and all he could hear was the rhythm of his gasps."[7] Joseph's intent was to swim until he was so tired that he drowned. Fortunately, bystanders saw him in the water and rescued him.

Over the next few weeks, during therapy sessions with Joseph, Haskell learned that the boy had been worrying obsessively. He fretted about whether he would ever grow taller. He wondered whether he would be able to take a girl to his family's tiny apartment where he slept with his brother in the living room on a foldout sofa. He worried about everything, and could not control it. No matter what he did, he was consumed by fear, dread, and a sense of hopelessness. Says Haskell: "Joseph was suffering from an anxiety disorder that had pushed him to a dangerous brink."[8]

Good Versus Bad Anxiety

When Haskell and other mental health professionals talk about anxiety disorders, they are referring to a group of conditions that are intense and prolonged, involving severe agitation and worrying. Although the exact prevalence is not known, as many as 30 percent of young people suffer from one or more anxiety disorders. According to a January 2016 Pew Research Center survey, anxiety disorders are more common among teenage girls than among boys (30.1 percent versus 20.3 percent).

As serious as anxiety disorders can be, and as much suffering as they cause, anxiety itself is not bad. It is a normal and natural human response to stress. Defined as feelings of worry, nervousness, or unease, anxiety alerts people to danger or potential threats. When they feel anxious (a derivative of the word *anxiety*), the stress hormones cortisol and adrenaline are released into the bloodstream. The heart rate speeds up, senses sharpen, and the person becomes more alert and focused, ready to make a quick decision whether to run from the threat or stay and deal with it. This is known as the fight-or-flight response.

Such anxiety is normal and is not at all the same as what plagues people with anxiety disorders. Their anxiety is severe, intense, and often debilitating; they live in a near-constant state of worry, fear, and dread. This can be agonizing for teens who are already coping with hormonal changes, peer pressures, school expectations, and other tough challenges that are part of growing up. Anita Amador saw the ongoing struggles of teens with anxiety disorders when she was interning at a high school support center. She talked with young people who were suffering, and she saw how much anxiety interfered with their lives. "Some students avoid going to class, can't concentrate on their work, or

Teens who suffer from anxiety disorders live in a near-constant state of worry and dread. This causes symptoms including the inability to concentrate and sleep disruptions that interfere with schoolwork.

have sleeping issues that impact their school work," says Amador. "Emotionally, they begin to alienate themselves from others, or not be interested in what they used to be interested in. Physically, they may not shower or keep up how they look, which is one of the first signs of anxiety and depression."[9]

Generalized Anxiety and Social Anxiety

One of the most common anxiety disorders among adolescents and young adults is generalized anxiety disorder. Young people with this disorder worry obsessively and excessively. For instance, most teens get stressed out at one time or another over exams. But someone with generalized anxiety disorder would not just experience stress; he or she would be consumed by fear and

A Superstar's Painful Revelation

Stefani Germanotta, better known as Lady Gaga, has been open about her struggles with mental illness and its effects on her life. In December 2016, in a letter posted to her Born This Way Foundation website, she revealed her longtime battle with PTSD. She talked about years of suffering with chronic pain and having no idea what was causing it. She also discussed her ongoing struggle to control her nervous system, which helps her avoid panicking over situations that would not necessarily bother other people. "Examples," she says, "are leaving the house or being touched by strangers who simply want to share their enthusiasm for my music."

There are times, Lady Gaga admits, when she cannot keep her severe anxiety under control. "It's like the panic accelerator in my mind gets stuck and I am paralyzed with fear," she says. When this happens, the effects are profound, as she explains: "It makes me have a common PTSD reaction which is that I feel depressed and unable to function like I used to. It's harder to do my job. It's harder to do simple things like take a shower. Everything has become harder." Because of what she has gone through and continues to endure, Lady Gaga has vowed to do all she can to help young people who are suffering. "I seek to raise awareness that this mental illness affects all kinds of people," she says, "including our youth."

Lady Gaga, "'Head Stuck in a Cycle I Look Off and I Stare': A Personal Letter from Gaga," Born This Way Foundation, December 6, 2016. https://bornthisway.foundation.

dread to the point of being physically sick. Such obsessive worrying may involve what psychologists call catastrophizing, which is imagining the worst possible outcome. Such imagined scenarios often extend well into the future. A teen with generalized anxiety disorder, for instance, might fear that a bad exam score would lead to such anger on the part of his or her parents that they would refuse to pay for college, which in turn would lead to the teen's unemployment, and thus ruin his or her life.

This hyperexaggerated fear is familiar to Sara Kidman, a college student who has suffered from generalized anxiety disorder for several years. She is plagued by the overwhelming dread that something bad will happen to her family or friends at home while she is not there. She describes irrational thoughts, incessant worry, a pounding heart, and night sweats. At school, says Kidman, "just like many students, you can bet my heart is racing and my hands are sweaty before an exam." But hers is not a temporary reaction—it is her day-to-day reality. "It's the days nobody else feels that way, when I still do," she says, adding:

> The days when I feel like I'm either going to pass out, throw up, or lose control of my bladder if I don't get up to leave the classroom. . . . The days I have to put lavender essential oil on my nose and focus on deep breathing more than on my professor's lecture just to make it through class. It's the days I sometimes can't push through and have to leave early—my friends know I'm struggling, but my peers surely view it as lazy. It's the days when my friend tries to comfort me by asking what's rolling through my head, but I can't come up with a response. Nothing—I have nothing to be anxious about. I just am.[10]

The deep, intense fear that is characteristic of generalized anxiety disorder also applies to social anxiety disorder, or social phobia. But this disorder revolves around the fear of interacting with others. People with social anxiety disorder have an intense, irrational dread of social situations, which is rooted in their fear of being observed, judged, and ultimately rejected. "People are social animals, and we have a strong desire to be part of a group and to be accepted by the group," says Stefan G. Hofmann, director of the Social Anxiety Program at Boston University. "Social anxiety is a result of the fear of a possibility that we will not be accepted by our peers. It's the fear of negative evaluation by others, and that is [part of] a very fundamental, biological need

"Social anxiety is a result of the fear of a possibility that we will not be accepted by our peers."[11]

—Stefan G. Hofmann, director of the Social Anxiety Program at Boston University to be liked."[11] Hofmann goes on to say that some social anxiety is natural and perfectly normal—just part of being human. It becomes a problem when the anxiety is so overpowering it interferes with someone's life and relationships.

Panic Disorder

Of all the anxiety disorders that are known to exist, panic disorder is among the most terrifying for sufferers. This mental illness is so named because its primary characteristic is sudden, inexplicable bouts of terror known as panic attacks. These are unpredictable, striking at any time, without warning, anywhere the person happens to be—even while he or she is sleeping. The attacks typically last from ten to fifteen minutes, although for the sufferer, it feels like they are going to last forever. Mental health experts say that the fear and dread of having an attack can sometimes be even more debilitating than the panic attacks themselves. When someone has a panic attack, frightening physical changes occur in the body that can be mistaken for a heart attack. People have described effects such as a racing heart, dizziness or lightheadedness, and breathing problems. Panic attacks may also cause difficulty swallowing, hot or cold flashes, chest pain, uncontrollable trembling, and feelings of nausea or intestinal distress. "Sounds nasty, right?" asks psychotherapist Natasha Daniels. "It doesn't feel good either. Trust me, I know." When Daniels started college, she was plagued by panic attacks, and she says they ruined her freshman year. "I didn't know what they were or what was happening to me,"[12] she says.

Hannah Hilgeman, a teenager from Ohio, has panic attacks several times a day. These happen at different times and in all kinds of places, from walking through the hallways at her high school to driving down the road, sitting in class, or watching movies at home on Netflix. "No place is safe from the monsters lurking around every corner," says Hilgeman. She can tell when a panic attack is about to strike, although she can do nothing to stop it—and the experience is terrifying. "I start to feel numb," she says. "I feel in danger, threatened, targeted, unsafe. I feel anxious. . . . While everyone else around me works peacefully on their homework assignment, I gasp for breath at an attempt to prove to myself I am still alive. I feel an incredible amount of fear, as if someone is pointing a gun right at me. This feeling of terror explains the tears beginning to form in my eyes."[13]

A Tough Combination

Hilgeman not only has panic disorder, she also suffers from depression. Although it is not common knowledge, this is true of many young people with mental illness. Depression, which is one of the mood disorders, is characterized by deep sadness, despair, and hopelessness. As different as that appears to be from anxiety-related conditions, the disorders are more closely related than many people think. "There is no evidence one disorder causes the other, but there is clear evidence that many people suffer from both disorders,"[14] says the Anxiety and Depression Association of America.

Sixteen-year-old Jeneisha Janice suffers from both anxiety and depression, and dealing with these mental illnesses makes life especially challenging for her. "As if being a teenager isn't hard enough," she says, "fighting two mental disorders doesn't make it a walk in the park." In the past, Janice has not spoken about her battle with mental illness, because she was embarrassed. "Some days I feel ashamed to be living with it," she says. "I have thoughts in my head saying, 'Why can't you be just like a normal person?' 'You're a burden to everyone.'"[15] Janice has been working on being more outspoken about her battle with anxiety and depression, which she hopes will help other young sufferers not feel so alone.

> "As if being a teenager isn't hard enough, fighting two mental disorders doesn't make it a walk in the park."[15]
>
> —Sixteen-year-old Jeneisha Janice, who suffers from anxiety and depression

Teen Depression Is Increasing

Depression is a serious mental illness that causes deep sadness, despair, and hopelessness. A study published in November 2016 revealed a 37 percent increase (between 2005 and 2014) in the number of young people who reported having a major depressive episode. The study also showed that depression is consistently more common among girls than boys. Study participants included 172,495 adolescents between the ages of twelve and seventeen.

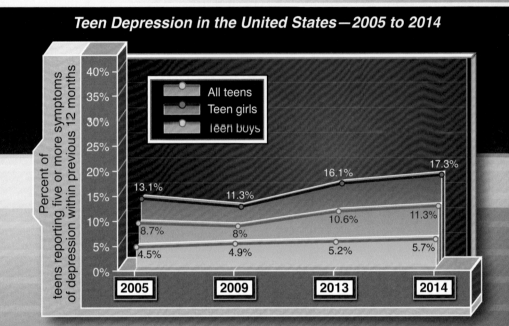

Teen Depression in the United States—2005 to 2014

Percent of teens reporting five or more symptoms of depression within previous 12 months

Legend:
- All teens
- Teen girls
- Teen boys

	2005	2009	2013	2014
Teen girls	13.1%	11.3%	16.1%	17.3%
All teens	8.7%	8%	10.6%	11.3%
Teen boys	4.5%	4.9%	5.2%	5.7%

Source: Ramin Mojtabai et al., "National Trends in the Prevalence and Treatment of Depression in Adolescents and Young Adults," *Pediatrics*, November 2016. http://pediatrics.aappublications.org.

Another teenage girl who suffers from anxiety and depression is Bailey Kay from Salt Lake City, Utah. She was diagnosed with an anxiety disorder in the seventh grade and with depression in the ninth grade. Since anxiety had troubled her since she was a child, the anxiety disorder diagnosis was no surprise to Kay. Hearing that she also had depression was surprising, however. She had been sadder than usual but assumed it was just part of being a teenager—an unfortunate but common misconception. The difference between typical teenage moodiness and depression is profound. Whereas normal moodiness leads to short-term sadness, anger, and crankiness, major depression produces deep, dark despair and hopelessness and sometimes the feeling that life no longer has meaning. These feelings can drag on for days, which seriously disrupts a young sufferer's ability to function.

Alarming, Growing Prevalence

Before Kay learned that she suffered from depression, she had begun showing symptoms—but did not recognize them as such. There was the characteristic sadness and despair: "I was crying over the stupidest things,"[16] she says. Kay was also eating too much and having trouble sleeping, both of which are common signs of depression in teens. Other warning signs include a lack of enthusiasm or motivation, constant tiredness with low to no energy, withdrawal from friends and family, poor self-esteem, feelings of worthlessness, uncharacteristic anger, overreaction to criticism, poor performance in school, and sometimes a preoccupation with death and dying.

Recent studies have shown an alarming trend: The incidence of depression among young people is growing fast. According to a November 2016 national survey, more than 11 percent of teens reported symptoms indicative of depression in 2014—a 37 percent spike over 2005. Separate documentation from the US Department of Health and Human Services (HHS) states that nearly one-third of teens in the United States have symptoms of depression, and millions of teens have depression severe enough to interfere with their daily functioning. Also according to the HHS, rates of depression among adolescent girls were more than double that of boys during 2015. This is consistent with the November 2016 study, which found that 17 percent of girls suffered from depression, compared with 6 percent of boys. Researchers are not sure why girls suffer from depression at rates nearly triple that of boys, and this is a topic of interest for ongoing depression studies.

Driven by Fears and Doubts

OCD is much less common among young people than depression and anxiety disorders. An estimated 1 percent to 3 percent of children and adolescents in the United States suffer from OCD, compared with 20 percent with anxiety disorders and 11.3 percent with depression. Yet OCD affects tens of thousands of youth in the United States and is a serious, debilitating mental illness. It typically starts developing during childhood, and if left untreated, it grows progressively worse.

Young OCD sufferers are tormented by obsessions, worries, and bad thoughts that will not go away. Accompanying these are compulsions, the persistent, uncomfortable urges to do certain things exactly right. This might include opening and closing a door exactly five or ten times, counting the steps from one room to another, or washing hands over and over and over again until they are red and raw.

These and other compulsive rituals are painfully familiar to Alisha Gregg, a teenage girl who suffers from OCD. She is plagued by intrusive thoughts, which is another characteristic of the disorder. Intrusive thoughts are unwanted ideas, often disturbing and frightening, that pop into someone's head throughout the day. Gregg offers a scenario, including the compulsions she relies on in a futile attempt to get rid of the troubling thoughts: "Walk down the stairs. Each step provokes a violent image. Tap four times. You're safe. OK, next step. Violent. violent, violent image. Stop. Stop. Stop. Stop. Stop. Nausea. Pounding heart. Tap. Tap. Tap. Tap. Breathe. *It's OK. I tapped. It's fine.* But, what if it's not?"[17]

Haunted by Trauma

The mental illness known as post-traumatic stress disorder (PTSD) is part of a psychiatric group called "trauma- and stressor-related disorders." The word *trauma* is germane to understanding PTSD because the condition develops as the result of living through

Battling Stereotypes

Kelly McNamara is a young woman living with the miserable effects of OCD. Because the illness causes her so much distress, it annoys her to hear people laughingly use the phrase "I'm so OCD" when complaining about a need for perfection or quest for neatness. "I can't help but wish to correct them," she says. "I know it's not their fault—the media has a lot to do with this false portrayal—but it still bothers me." She might hear, for instance, "I'm so OCD" when a friend finds it impossible to do homework unless the floor is clean, insists on always being punctual, cannot stand having her hair not look perfect, or gets stressed out if someone knocks her perfectly organized stack of books over. In comparison, says McNamara, real OCD can be "torturous." She writes:

> Oh my God, my car just ran over a bump. I know it's a pothole, but what if it's not? Should I go back and check? I have to look in the rear view mirror a few times. Just in case, I need to knock on the window a couple times. Two times exactly. I still feel anxious, because even though I know I didn't hit someone, what if I did? Am I a bad person? How can I know? I should never drive again.

Kelly McNamara, "How My OCD Isn't like Someone Saying 'I'm So OCD,'" *The Mighty* (blog), August 28, 2015. https://themighty.com.

a traumatic experience. This can happen to anyone, including adults, children, and teenagers, and is not limited to military veterans, as many people believe. "If you mention PTSD," says Naomi Moresi, who suffers from the disorder, "the first image that comes to mind is a war veteran who experiences the horror of combat. However, many people can develop PTSD from less severe experiences, like motor vehicle accidents."[18]

Moresi specifically cites motor vehicle accidents because a serious car wreck is what led to her developing PTSD when she was a teenager. She was sixteen and had gotten her driver's license only six days before the wreck. Her car was totaled, as was the other car involved in the crash. She says the experience was so traumatic for her that it sent her "into a spiral of PTSD."

Moresi was filled with anxiety every time she got into a car. Her heart raced out of control even in a parking lot. After two more minor accidents, her trauma worsened, and she stopped driving altogether. Her grades started slipping, and she could not sleep at night. "Not understanding what was happening, I felt bad all the time,"[19] she says.

Along with motor vehicle crashes, other types of trauma that have been associated with PTSD include being a victim of sexual abuse or rape; physical abuse; natural disasters such as hurricanes, tornadoes, earthquakes, or floods; human-made disasters such as a fire; and violent crimes such as kidnapping or school shootings. Health officials also state that PTSD can develop after someone has witnessed violence; such events may include domestic violence in the home, community violence, terrorist attacks, or war.

Disordered Eating

All mental illnesses make life difficult for young people because the effects of these illnesses cause so much distress. This is certainly the case with eating disorders such as anorexia (anorexia nervosa) and bulimia (bulimia nervosa). These serious conditions affect people of all ages but mostly develop during adolescence. They affect females more often than males, but anyone can develop an eating disorder. Although anorexia and bulimia have very different characteristics, they share one trait in common: dysfunctional, unhealthy relationships with food that can lead to severe health problems.

Anorexia is characterized by distorted body image, the quest for a perfect body (and often perfection in general), and a deep fear of being fat. Teens in the throes of anorexia eat so little and take in so few calories that they literally starve themselves. Mental health professionals who specialize in eating disorders say that anorexia is the most deadly of all mental illnesses, with about half of anorexia-related deaths resulting from suicide. According to Nancy Zucker, a professor of psychology and neuroscience at Duke University, many disorders involve irrational or dysfunc-

Although they can develop in people of any age, eating disorders are most common among adolescents. One of these disorders is anorexia nervosa, whose sufferers deeply fear being overweight and eat so little that they literally starve themselves.

tional behavior, but in anorexia, she says, "individuals are basically starving themselves to death. You don't have to be a scientist to step back and say there's something horribly wrong here."[20] A number of severe, life-threatening health risks are associated with anorexia, including heart failure, kidney failure, pancreatitis (inflammation of the pancreas), osteoporosis (premature bone deterioration), and a number of other diseases and disorders.

Bulimia is also life-threatening, and like anorexia it is associated with numerous severe health problems. But it is different from anorexia in that young people with bulimia do not count calories and ration tiny bits of food. Rather, they eat massive amounts of food and then attempt to get rid of it by purging their bodies of the calories they have consumed. This usually involves forcing themselves to vomit by sticking their fingers down their throats—and young bulimia sufferers may vomit ten times a day or even more frequently.

One bulimia sufferer is a young woman named Celine Sauve. She has overheard people make remarks about self-induced vomiting, saying how horrible it must be to do that after every meal. "What they don't understand," says Sauve, "is that's the easy part for me." She goes on to explain the mental anguish that is far worse for her than frequent vomiting: "The ghost of bulimia doesn't just come out for a short visit after meals. It doesn't go back into hiding once its job is done. The ghost of bulimia is a constant, negative force that controls my every sense, my every emotion and my every thought of every second of every day."[21]

Experts are not exactly sure how many teens suffer from eating disorders, because so many of them never seek treatment. According to a 2017 article on the website WebMD, research suggests that more than one-third of adolescent girls believe they are overweight, and a much higher number want to lose weight. Unfortunately, too many young people opt to lose that weight in extremely unhealthy ways—and are risking their lives in the process.

> "The ghost of bulimia is a constant, negative force that controls my every sense, my every emotion and my every thought of every second of every day."[21]
>
> —Celine Sauve, a young woman who suffers from bulimia

Troubled Teens

From out-of-control anxiety to depression, OCD, PTSD, and eating disorders, millions of young people are plagued by mental illness. This can cause a great deal of distress, especially since they are already trying to cope with raging hormones, academic expectations, and the seemingly endless stream of challenges that go along with being a teen. Although no one can make mental illness disappear, family members, teachers, and friends can show compassion and a willingness to listen. By doing so, they can make life a little more bearable for those who are suffering.

Chapter 2

What Causes Mental Illness?

A s far as Nina Langton was concerned, she had no reason to feel depressed. The pretty, popular teenage girl lived in an affluent neighborhood in Bolton, Connecticut, and enjoyed a close, loving relationship with her parents. She was a talented athlete who had many great friends. She seemed to have everything going for her. Yet she was burdened by sadness and did not know why. "Part of what made my depression so difficult," says Langton, "is that I didn't understand why I was feeling so sad."[22]

Multiple Causes

Langton's confusion about her feelings is typical of young people with depression and other mental illnesses. It can be frustrating to be diagnosed with one of these disorders and even worse to hear that no one knows the cause. Unfortunately, that is the reality of mental illness. Even though scientists have learned a great deal through research, they cannot say for sure what causes it or why some people develop it when most do not. "One of the cruel things about mental illness is how randomly it can strike," says *New York* magazine editor Jesse Singal. "There's often no rhyme or reason to it: Some people endure almost unfathomable trauma but are subsequently quite 'normal' in their day-to-day functioning, while other people develop crippling mental-health issues despite a lack of known risk factors."[23]

A widely accepted belief about mental illness is that there is no single cause. Rather, multiple factors likely work together in complex ways to cause depression, anxiety disorders, OCD, and other mental illnesses. "A mental health condition isn't the result of one event," says NAMI. "Research suggests multiple, linking causes. Genetics, environment and lifestyle influence whether someone develops a mental health condition."[24]

Family History

One of the most consistent research findings about mental illness is the prominent role of genetics (meaning heredity). Studies of identical twins—and children of parents with mental illness—have shown that there is a genetic component to mental illness. So if one or both parents suffer from depression, their children have a higher-than-average likelihood of also having it. This does not mean they are certain to develop the disorder, but their chances are greater than someone without a family history. "Children born into families with a history of highly genetic mental illnesses . . . have a vulnerability to the illness in every cell of their body," says Diane McIntosh, a psychiatrist from British Columbia, Canada. She adds that much is still unknown about the connection between genes and mental illness. "We haven't figured out precisely which genes are responsible for mental illnesses," says McIntosh, "but scientists have identified many 'candidate genes' that are likely involved."[25]

> "Children born into families with a history of highly genetic mental illnesses . . . have a vulnerability to the illness in every cell of their body."[25]
>
> —Diane McIntosh, a psychiatrist from British Columbia, Canada

A Complex Combination

Scientists believe that there is no one cause for mental illness: Rather, a number of factors work together. These include biological, psychological, and environmental factors.

Mental Illness

Genetics (Heredity)	Family history of mental illness
Brain chemistry	Impaired function or imbalance of chemicals known as neurotransmitters
Exposures before birth	Toxins, alcohol or drug use by mother
Environmental/ Lifestyle	Traumatic experience, child abuse or neglect, stressful living situation (poverty, family conflict), use of alcohol and/or drugs

Source: Mayo Clinic, "Mental Illness Causes," October 13, 2015. www.mayoclinic.org.

One mental illness with strong genetic ties is schizophrenia, which is a severe, crippling brain disorder. For young people with a parent or sibling who has schizophrenia, the risk of developing it is about ten times that of youth with no family history. The illness most often develops between ages fifteen and twenty-five. Its defining characteristic is psychosis, which is the terrifying state of losing one's grip on reality. During psychotic breaks, people with schizophrenia may suffer from delusions, which are beliefs and ideas that are not true: "Everyone in the whole school hates me and wants to hurt me" is an example of a delusion. Psychosis can also result in hallucinations, which involve hearing voices or seeing things that are not really there.

In July 2014 the largest schizophrenia study of all time was published in the scientific journal *Nature*, and its findings were significant. The researchers studied genetic data to search for genes that were associated with the illness. They found 108 different genes that were directly linked to schizophrenia. This removed any lingering doubt about the illness's association with genetics and was considered a breakthrough finding. Still, the researchers emphasize that many more genes will likely be identified before schizophrenia's genetic links are fully understood. "Now we have 108 pieces," says psychiatric researcher Steven Hyman, "but maybe it's a 1,000-piece puzzle, so we have a long way to go."[26]

Nature and Nurture

Although genetics is a known contributor to many types of mental illness, genes alone cannot cause these illnesses. If other factors were not involved, everyone with a family history of mental illness would develop it, and most do not. Thus, scientists are convinced that mental illness results from a complex interaction between genetic vulnerability and environmental (or external) factors. Certain genes, for example, may increase a teen's susceptibility to developing mental illness, and factors related to his or her life situation may trigger its onset.

This phenomenon of genetic and environmental factors coming together to cause mental illness is often referred to as nature versus nurture. "The nature-nurture debate is concerned with the relative contribution that both influences make to human behavior,"[27] says Saul McLeod, a psychology researcher with the University of Manchester in Manchester, England. Nature, he explains, involves brain chemistry, genetics, and other natural biological factors. Nurture generally refers to all external factors that affect someone after birth.

Through years of research, scientists have identified numerous environmental factors that may play a role in the development of mental illness. In this case "environment" can have a very broad

Possible Link Between Psychosis and Pot

Teenagers are often warned about the dangers of drugs and alcohol. If they knew these substances could potentially cause brain damage, they might be more likely to heed the warning. During adolescence, the human brain has not yet finished developing; brain development is not complete until about age twenty-five. Thus, teens are far more vulnerable than adults to damage that can lead to mental illness.

According to Dost Öngür, a psychiatrist who specializes in psychotic disorders, teens who smoke marijuana have a risk of developing schizophrenia that is three times higher than teens who do not use the drug. "Kids who are smoking daily are at the highest risk," says Öngür. "Kids smoking on weekends but not every day are at somewhat lower risk. And kids who are not smoking at all are at the lowest risk." Öngür is aware that his stance on teens and pot smoking is controversial. He acknowledges that there is a great deal of mystery about what causes mental illness. "We don't have a special microscope that looks into people's minds," he says. Still, Öngür warns, if teens do not want to risk developing a debilitating psychotic mental illness, they should stay away from marijuana.

Quoted in Carey Goldberg, "Leading Psychosis Expert to His Students: To Avoid Risk, Hold Off on Pot Til 30," *CommonHealth*, October 21, 2016. www.wbur.org.

meaning; exposure to toxins before birth is an environmental risk factor, as is an unhappy family life, death or divorce in the family, chronic (long-lasting) stress, severe bullying, feelings of inadequacy, or enduring a traumatic experience such as being the victim of a violent crime or living through a natural or human-made disaster.

Living in poverty also raises the risk of mental illness because young people must cope with a great deal of stress. Research clearly shows that youths from low-income families, those who live in foster care, and those who live in high-crime neighborhoods all have an elevated risk for mental illness. According to US government data, 21 percent of low-income children and youth aged six to seventeen have mental illnesses. Among those in the child welfare system, 50 percent suffer from mental health disorders. Psychiatrist Rob Haskell writes: "The most socioeconomically disadvantaged children have always lived with excessive stress: unsafe neighborhoods, inconsistent sources of food and shelter, few routes out of cyclic poverty."[28]

Another significant contributing factor to mental illness is child abuse. When young children are hurt by the very people they count on for love, support, and nurturing, it can cause irreparable harm and potentially lead to the development of mental illness later in life. Research has shown, for instance, that the severe stress and psychological pain associated with child abuse can cause brain damage; specifically, to a region of the brain known as the hippocampus. This part of the brain helps with creating new memories, storing long-term memories, and controlling the body's reactions to emotions and stress. If the hippocampus is damaged, this can affect the child's ability to cope with stress later in life. "In other words," says neuroscience journalist Maia Szalavitz, "early stress makes the brain less resilient to the effects of later stress."[29]

A 2012 study by researchers from Harvard University strengthened prior theories about brain damage from child abuse. Nearly two hundred young adults aged eighteen to twenty-five participated in the study. Brain scans of those who suffered abuse as children showed noticeable changes in key regions in and around the hippocampus. About 25 percent had gone on to develop depression, and 7 percent developed PTSD. The researchers also learned that the incidence of mental illness was closely associated with the severity of abuse. For example, among participants who had suffered three or more types of child maltreatment (such as physical abuse, neglect, and verbal abuse), 53 percent had developed depression, and 40 percent had developed PTSD. In the final report, the study authors conclude: "Childhood maltreatment or abuse is a major risk factor for mood, anxiety, substance abuse, psychotic, and personality disorders."[30]

Remarkable Yet Vulnerable

Studying the brain has been and continues to be a high priority for scientists who pursue mental illness research. The human brain is

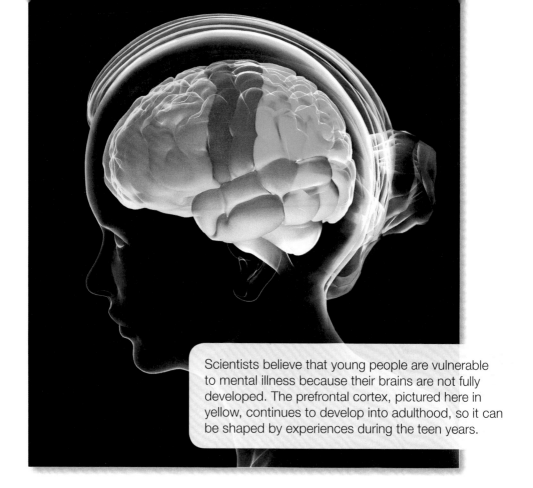

Scientists believe that young people are vulnerable to mental illness because their brains are not fully developed. The prefrontal cortex, pictured here in yellow, continues to develop into adulthood, so it can be shaped by experiences during the teen years.

an amazingly complex organ whose function relies on an intricate network of cells known as neurons. These cells, which number somewhere around 100 billion, send and receive messages in the form of rapid-fire electrical signals. This constant communication is facilitated by brain chemicals known as neurotransmitters. Cornell University's medical school, Weill Cornell Medicine, refers to this process as "a dance of chemical messages so delicate that missteps often lead to neurological dysfunction."[31] If this "dance" (meaning brain chemistry) is disrupted in any way, the brain cannot work properly. This may result in everything from mood swings and insomnia to mild or severe mental illness.

Young people are especially vulnerable to mental illness because their brains are not fully developed. In the past, scientists believed that brain development was complete before children entered adolescence. That was shown to be incorrect in the late twentieth century. Researchers discovered that dramatic changes

Social Media and Anxiety

Today's teens are attached to their smartphones—so much so that many could not imagine being without one. They use their phones for everything from texting friends and taking photos to checking their favorite social media apps. As indispensable as these gadgets are, mental health experts have grown increasingly concerned about a possible link between excessive use and mental illnesses such as anxiety and depression. According to a 2017 survey, some of the most popular social media apps are harmful to young people's mental health and well-being.

Nearly fifteen hundred young people aged fourteen to twenty-four took part in the survey. They were asked to share, from their personal experience, the effects of five different social media platforms on certain health-related issues. Some of these were loneliness, sleep, self-identity, body image, depression, anxiety, bullying, and the fear of missing out. From what the young people shared, Instagram is perceived as the most damaging, followed by Snapchat, Facebook, and Twitter (in that order). Although YouTube was said to interfere with sleep, it was the only social media app that had a positive impact on youth. Shirley Cramer, chief executive of the group that conducted the survey, was not surprised that Instagram and Snapchat were ranked as the worst for mental health and well-being. "Both platforms are very image-focused," she says, "and it appears that they may be driving feelings of inadequacy and anxiety in young people."

Quoted in Denis Campbell, "Facebook and Twitter 'Harm Young People's Mental Health,'" *Guardian* (Manchester), May 19, 2017. https://amp.theguardian.com.

occur in the brain during the teenage years and development is not complete until around age twenty-five.

The last part of the brain to develop is the prefrontal cortex, which is at the very front of the brain, behind the forehead. This part of the brain is associated with executive functions such as judgment, decision making, problem solving, planning and prioritizing, evaluation of risks, regulation of emotion, and "the ability to change plans when faced with an obstacle," says McGill University psychiatry professor Cecilia Flores. She adds that because the prefrontal cortex continues to develop into adulthood, it is particularly susceptible to being shaped by teenagers' life experiences, including stress and drug abuse. "Such alterations in pre-frontal cortex development can have long term consequences later on in life,"[32] says Flores.

Eating Disorder Mysteries

One group of mental illnesses that research has tied to brain chemistry is eating disorders like anorexia and bulimia. These disorders are typically associated with external factors, including the media's constant depiction of perfect bodies, society's emphasis on thinness, and stressful or traumatic occurrences that could potentially trigger dysfunctional beliefs about food. These are all important factors, according to Walter Kaye, a physician from San Diego, California, who specializes in eating disorders. But evidence is growing that the real origination of these disorders is in the brain. "Lots of people diet or want to lose weight," says Kaye, "but relatively few of them end up with anorexia nervosa or bulimia nervosa. . . . Culture plays some role—but maybe less so than we thought in the past."[33]

Eating disorders are mystifying to scientists for a number of reasons. One puzzling aspect of these disorders is that they affect females far more often than males. It is widely assumed that males make up about 10 percent of those affected by anorexia and bulimia. Yet scientists are starting to question the accuracy of this statistic. Perhaps males are not counted in the totals of eating disorder sufferers because they rarely reach out for help. Or research findings could possibly be skewed because studies almost exclusively focus on females.

> "Lots of people diet or want to lose weight, but relatively few of them end up with anorexia nervosa or bulimia nervosa."[33]
>
> —Walter Kaye, a physician from San Diego, California

One young man who suffered from anorexia and waited a long time before telling anyone is Zayn Malik, formerly of the band One Direction. "Something I've never talked about in public before, but which I have come to terms with since leaving the band, is that I was suffering from an eating disorder," he says. "I'd just go for days—sometimes two or three days straight—without eating anything at all. It got quite serious, although at the time I didn't recognize it for what it was."[34] Malik lost so much weight that he became sick, and he was also suffering from anxiety attacks. Now, several years later, he is feeling much healthier. He attributes his struggle with food to feeling that he was not in control of his life. Food, he says, was something he could control—so he did, even though he now knows his way of controlling food was harmful.

The Gender Factor

The prevalence of other types of mental illnesses may also vary by gender, including anxiety disorders. Both males and females suffer from them, but during the teenage years, they are about twice as common among girls. The same is true of depression, which affects girls far more often than boys. Although scientists cannot pinpoint the reasons for this disparity, they strongly suspect that brain chemistry is involved. Brain scans have shown differences in how girls and boys process emotional stimuli, as physician Ron J. Steingard, who is medical director for Child Mind Institute, explains: "Girls mature, in terms of their emotional recognition, faster than boys—and that sensitivity could make them more vulnerable to depression and anxiety."[35]

Brain chemistry is at the root of another theory about why girls have anxiety disorders and depression more than boys. According to the Anxiety and Depression Association of America, the brain system involved in the fight-or-flight response is activated differently in females. Also, the female hormones estrogen and progesterone may play a role in the frequency of females developing depression and anxiety disorders, although the exact mechanisms by which this occurs are not well understood.

A study published in 2017 focused on teen depression during the period from 2005 to 2014. Public health researchers wanted to see whether prevalence of the disorder increased over that time, and they found that it had—dramatically. And not only had depression's prevalence soared, nearly three-fourths of the depressed teens were girls. Psychologist and study author Catherine Steiner-Adair was not at all surprised to learn that so many girls suffer from depression. She says that young women are continuously "bombarded by media messages, dominant culture, humor and even political figures about how they look—no matter how smart, gifted, or passionate they are."[36]

Another gender-related disparity is how traumatic stress affects males and females differently. Studies involving girls and boys who have lived through trauma have found that girls are more likely than boys to develop PTSD. A 2016 study by researchers from the Stanford University School of Medicine may help explain why this is so. The researchers conducted magnetic resonance imaging (MRI) scans on the brains of fifty-nine participants aged nine to seventeen, of whom thirty (fourteen girls and sixteen boys) had PTSD. The scans showed structural differences between girls and boys in the insula, a small region of the brain that is about the size of a prune. "The insula appears to play a key role in the development of PTSD,"[37] says Victor Carrion, senior author of the study.

The insula's function is to detect cues from the body and then process emotions and empathy. Abnormal changes could interfere with the insula's ability to function properly. Thus, differences in the girls' insulas (as shown in the MRIs) could possibly explain why girls have a more difficult time coping with trauma. "The difference we saw between the brains of boys and girls who have experienced psychological trauma is important," says Carrion, "because it may help explain differences in trauma symptoms between sexes."[38] He emphasizes the need for additional studies of young people who have suffered trauma and developed PTSD.

Stress Overload

Experts also emphasize the need for research into the dramatic rise of depression and anxiety disorders in teens. Many mental health professionals are convinced that a factor in the increase

Depression and anxiety disorders have risen dramatically among teens in recent decades. Some researchers attribute this in part to teens' seeming inability to escape the relentless bombardment of negative information that they might receive through social media and other online activities.

is the stress on young people, which can be overwhelming. On top of a long school day that typically starts early in the morning, teens are loaded down with homework, pressured to get the best grades, and strongly encouraged to be involved in sports and other extracurricular activities. According to Arizona State University psychology professor Suniya Luthar, the single biggest stressor for these youth is never reaching the point of being able to say they have done enough and can ease up on themselves. She explains: "There's always one more activity, one more A.P. class, one more thing to do in order to get into a top college. Kids have a sense that they're not measuring up. The pressure is relentless and getting worse."[39]

Pressure and stress became overwhelming for Jake, a young man from North Carolina. During his junior year in high school, Jake excelled in everything he did. He was taking three Advanced Placement classes, earned stellar grades, and was a runner with his school's cross-country team. He also participated in the Model United Nations program, in which students learn about diplomacy, international relations, and the United Nations. On the outside Jake appeared to be handling his jam-packed schedule just fine, but on the inside the pressure was building. Finally, the stress became too much, and Jake just shut down. He did not want to go to school, he developed migraine headaches, and he felt like nothing he did was good enough. "All of a sudden I couldn't do anything," he says. "I was so afraid."[40] That was the beginning of Jake's long, painful battle with anxiety and depression.

As tough as school-related stress can be, psychologist Janis Whitlock is not convinced it is the main driver of the teen depression and anxiety epidemic. Rather, she blames the constant bombardment of information that is coming at kids from social media and other online activity. Whitlock refers to this as a "cauldron of stimulus they can't get away from, or don't want to get away from, or don't know how to get away from."[41] Because teens spend so much time online, they are pummeled with news and opinions about everything from sexism and racism to climate change and political upheaval.

Faith-Ann Bishop, a young woman from Hermon, Maine, suffered from debilitating anxiety throughout middle school and high school. She has a perspective that is similar to Whitlock's. "We're the first generation that cannot escape our problems at all," says Bishop. "We're all like little volcanoes. We're getting this constant pressure, from our phones, from our relationships, from the way things are today."[42]

> "We're the first generation that cannot escape our problems at all. We're all like little volcanoes. We're getting this constant pressure, from our phones, from our relationships, from the way things are today."[42]
>
> —Faith-Ann Bishop, a young woman from Hermon, Maine

Technology and Social Media

The hyperconnectedness of today's young people is an issue of concern to mental health experts. As much as teens love and are attached to their smartphones, a growing number of experts think the gadgets may be linked to the sharp rise in teen depression and anxiety. One of these experts is Jean Twenge, a psychology professor at San Diego State University. To further explore this issue, Twenge gathered data collected between 2010 and 2015 from more than five hundred thousand adolescents throughout the United States. She found that young people who spent the most time daily on their smartphones (or other electronic devices) were significantly more likely to feel depressed and/or suicidal. Overall, teens who spent many hours daily on social media and little time engaging in in-person social interactions were the most likely to suffer from depression.

One college student has strong opinions about his generation's attachment to social media. "I don't think we realize how much it's affecting our moods and personalities," he says. "Social media is a tool, but it's become this thing that we can't live without but that's making us crazy." In his particular case, the young man has no doubt that social media has made him more self-conscious. "In high school, I'd constantly be judging my self-worth online," he says. As he thinks back to those years, he remembers how Facebook fueled his insecurity. "I would think, Oh, people don't want to see *me* on their timeline."[43]

Many Lingering Questions

Through the years, as scientists have learned more about mental illness, they have come up with a number of theories about causes. Generally, these disorders result from biological vulnerability such as genetics combined with multiple environmental factors. As the prevalence of depression and anxiety disorders has soared among young people, mental health experts have become concerned about the association between these conditions and increased use of electronics. Undoubtedly, future research will answer at least some of the questions that continue to mystify scientists.

Chapter 3

Can Mental Illness Be Treated or Cured?

Today young people with depression, anxiety disorders, PTSD, and other mental illnesses have more treatment options than ever before. These illnesses cannot be cured the way some physical ailments can be, and this is frustrating for anyone who suffers from them. But the right treatment can make a remarkable difference in how a young person feels. Teens who are treated can often manage their illness and keep symptoms under control. Rather than continuing to feel miserable and hopeless, they start feeling positive and better able to cope with life's ups and downs.

Before Caitlin Wren was treated for depression, she felt sad all the time, and she was also frightened about what might be wrong with her. "I don't think I've ever been so scared in my entire life," she wrote in her journal. On the advice of her therapist, Wren began journaling when she was fifteen. She started seeing him after confessing to her parents how terribly sad she felt and that she no longer enjoyed doing much of anything. Now nineteen,

Wren credits the therapy with saving her life. "If my parents hadn't been so great in getting me help and treatment right away, I probably, I definitely, would not be here today." Wren is now a college student and doing very well, as she explains: "I'm able to go to school, I'm able to go out and live a life and that is something that I never ever imagined that I would be able to do."[44]

Healing Through Therapy

Like Wren, many teens with mental illness view therapy as changing—and even saving—their lives. Because of how profoundly it can help ease suffering, therapy is a standard part of most mental illness treatment plans. By working with a trusted therapist in a safe environment, young people can open up about situations and feelings that are painful or troubling. They learn to be honest with the therapist—and with themselves—about what they are thinking and feeling. Over time they learn how to better manage their feelings and not let themselves get consumed by self-doubt and negativity.

"If my parents hadn't been so great in getting me help and treatment right away, I probably, I definitely, would not be here today."[44]

—Caitlin Wren, a young woman who was treated for depression as a teen

There are a number of different therapy methods, each with its own approach and techniques. A physician or mental health provider will recommend the best type of therapy for a patient's individual needs. Many patients participate in multiple kinds of therapy. Sessions may be held on an individual basis, where the therapist and patient meet one-on-one. Or a small group of teens with similar issues may get together for therapy sessions. By meeting as a group, they can work through their own problems, gain insight from others, and in turn offer suggestions and support to their fellow group members about their issues. "Young people who have difficulty with friendships or other relationships can often benefit from the social interactions that are a basic part

Many teens who suffer from mental illnesses find therapy to be of great benefit. One type is family therapy, in which family members learn skills that help them better communicate with each other and resolve conflicts.

of group therapy,"[45] says the Association for Children's Mental Health.

Family therapy involves not only the patient but also select family members, such as parents or siblings. This method is intended to help improve how a family communicates and functions together. It is based on the theory that when one family member has problems, the whole family has probably played some role in that. In other words, a teen's mental illness may be a symptom of a larger problem related to family relationships and dynamics. "It is possible," says physician Adam Husney, "that if the person with the illness is treated but the family is not, another member of the family will become ill. This cycle will continue until the problems are examined and treated."[46] During family therapy sessions, the therapist observes interactions between family members and looks for weaknesses and breakdowns, as well as strengths that can be built on. Family members learn skills to help them communicate

Pets Help Teens Heal

For young people suffering from mental illness, time spent with pets can be both enjoyable and beneficial. Research has shown that pet therapy can reduce anxiety levels more than other recreational activities. According to NAMI, pets provide a nonjudgmental form of interaction that can motivate and encourage people, especially children. Sessions with therapy pets may focus on goals from human-animal interaction, such as developing social skills or increasing self-esteem. Simply spending time holding a therapy pet can also lower anxiety levels.

Morgan Hubbard, a teenage girl from Des Moines, Iowa, credits pet therapy with saving her life. Hubbard had been bullied in school, suffered from severe social anxiety and depression, and had tried to commit suicide twice. As part of her treatment program, she became involved with the Jester Park Equestrian Center in Granger, Iowa, and immediately fell in love with horses. "They can tell when you're scared of them," she says—which she was at first. "They can tell when you're happy. They can tell when you're sad. And they react to that same thing." Hubbard's equine therapy has helped her so much that after volunteering at the center, she went to work there doing barn chores and working with clients. She plans to pursue a career in nursing so she can help other young people who also struggle with mental illness.

Quoted in Kim Norvell, "Teen Overcomes Depression with Help of Horses," *USA Today*, June 2, 2016. www.usatoday.com.

more effectively, reduce conflicts, and get through stressful times together even after therapy sessions come to an end.

Teens who suffer from bulimia can benefit more from family therapy than individual therapy, according to a 2015 study. Researchers from San Francisco, California, recruited 130 young people aged twelve to eighteen to participate in the study; all had been diagnosed with bulimia. Half were treated with family therapy, and the others with a method known as cognitive behavioral therapy, or CBT. At six- and twelve-month intervals, the teens who took part in family therapy had a much higher rate of recovery than those in the CBT group. This finding, says lead researcher Daniel Le Grange, contradicts a long-standing belief among physicians that parents should be excluded from therapy because they are to blame when a child develops bulimia. Le Grange adds: "Parents need to be actively involved in the treatment of kids and teens with eating disorders."[47] He notes that CBT can be effective in treating bulimia but says it does not work as well as family therapy.

Depression and Anxiety Treatment

CBT is, however, the preferred therapy for treating depression in teens. Developed by a psychiatrist during the 1960s, this therapy method focuses on helping young people radically change negative or destructive thought patterns. They become aware of how profoundly thoughts and feelings can influence their behaviors. They learn to recognize negative or unrealistic thoughts and to purposely change the direction of their thinking to become more realistic and positive. For instance, says NAMI, CBT can help a young patient replace negative thoughts that lead to low self-esteem, such as "I can't do anything right," with more positive expectations: "I can do this most of the time, based on my prior experiences."[48]

A subcategory of CBT, known as exposure therapy, is often used with patients suffering from anxiety disorders. Exposure therapy is so named because it helps people overcome their fears by being exposed to them—by facing them head-on. The thinking behind this approach is that when people are afraid of a particular object or situation, their natural reaction is to avoid it. But by doing that they will remain afraid, and their fears usually grow worse. Psychiatrist Rob Haskell got over his fear of flying not by avoiding air travel, but by flying as often as possible, "which was miserable until it wasn't," he says. The same principle applies to teens suffering

> "Parents need to be actively involved in the treatment of kids and teens with eating disorders."[47]
>
> —Daniel Le Grange, a psychologist who specializes in eating disorders

from an anxiety disorder. Exposure therapy, Haskell explains, involves "repeated, controlled exposure to the threat—whether it's spiders or school or speaking up."[49] Over time, the patient sees that what seemed so threatening and scary before may not be such a big deal after all.

Exposure therapy is not typically a pleasant experience for patients; there is nothing fun about forcing oneself to face frightening beliefs, memories, and situations. For sixteen-year-old Jillian, who was treated at a New Hampshire residential facility called Mountain Valley, exposure therapy was almost more than she could bear. She suffered from crippling anxiety, and one of her biggest fears was being ridiculed or rejected by other young people. This was rooted in her experience with severe cyberbullying in middle school.

The facility's staff enlisted young people who were also receiving treatment at Mountain Valley to assist in Jillian's therapy sessions. Their job was to voice her worst insecurities while Jillian listened to their comments. "I can't believe how insignificant Jillian is," one remarked. "I mean, for the first three weeks, I thought her name was Susan." Jillian held it together until one of the teens said, "If she left tomorrow, maybe we wouldn't even miss her." Tears welled up in Jillian's eyes, and she told the therapist she could not keep going. Exposure therapists do not push patients beyond their limits, and the therapist told Jillian she could stop if she wanted to. Jillian considered that option and then decided against it, saying, "No, I feel like I need to do this."[50] She realized that if she could not handle an uncomfortable session with her peers in the protected environment of Mountain Valley, she would certainly not be able to deal with the much harsher real world.

Tough but Effective

Exposure therapy is often used to treat teens with PTSD, and like Jillian, trauma survivors can find the experience almost unbearable. These young people have usually endured trauma such as physical abuse, sexual assault, a devastating accident, or a disastrous earthquake or fire. The last thing in the world these victims want to do is go through the horrific ordeal again—yet in a sense, that is what happens with exposure therapy. As unthinkable as it may seem, the approach has proved to work wonders for military veterans traumatized by the horrors of war, and it has had similar benefits for young PTSD sufferers.

University of Pennsylvania psychologist Edna Foa has studied the use of exposure therapy for young people who have been sexually abused. As part of her 2013 study, she recruited sixty-one teenage girls aged thirteen to eighteen who had sought help at a rape crisis center in Philadelphia, Pennsylvania. Each of them had been raped or sexually abused, sometimes repeatedly, often by a member of their own family. All the girls had developed PTSD as a result of the trauma.

For fourteen weeks one group of girls participated in traditional counseling, and the other group took part in exposure therapy. Sessions lasted for sixty to ninety minutes. Initially, most girls in the exposure therapy group became very upset when talking about their traumatic experiences. But by repeating the same account of that trauma over and over, says Foa, "they get a new perspective of what happened. They get used to thinking and talking about the memory and realizing that it was in the past, that it's not in the present anymore."[51] Eventually, the girls were able to distance themselves enough from their traumatic experiences that they felt a sense of closure.

The study showed remarkable results. At the end of the fourteen weeks, more than 80 percent of the girls in the exposure therapy group no longer fit the criteria for a PTSD diagnosis, compared with 54 percent of girls in the other group. Although Foa's approach had been criticized as being too extreme for young rape victims, supporters say the girls' recovery was strong evidence of the technique's effectiveness. In a December 2013 editorial, psychologist Sean Perrin, who specializes in PTSD treatment in kids, said the study "should allay therapist concerns about any potential harmful effects of exposure."[52] Perrin noted that that the distress that comes with reliving trauma usually goes away after a few sessions of exposure therapy and is an essential part of recovery.

Taming the Trauma

A therapy technique known as eye movement desensitization and reprocessing (EMDR) is nothing like exposure therapy, but it also has been effective at helping young people with PTSD. The complicated-sounding name describes a method that, aptly, in-

A woman undergoes eye movement desensitization and reprocessing (EMDR). This method for treating post-traumatic stress disorder involves the patient remembering the traumatic event while following a moving focal point with the eyes. In time, memories of the traumatic event take on less importance.

volves repeatedly moving one's eyes. Patients focus on thoughts of the traumatic experience, while following the therapist's hand with their eyes as it moves back and forth across the field of vision. To facilitate this eye movement, the therapist might wave a wand or small light back and forth. These eye movement exercises are repeated until the memories connected with the traumatic event begin to take on less and less importance.

EMDR therapy helped Kyler Erickson get his life back. In 2011, when he was a senior in high school, Erickson witnessed a deadly school shooting committed by one of his classmates. He was traumatized by the incident and plagued by terrifying nightmares and flashbacks long afterward. A year and a half later, he was still suffering terribly and sought professional help. After being diagnosed with PTSD, Erickson went through months of EMDR sessions. He sat in a darkened room with a therapist, and as a light board flashed different patterns in front of him, he forced himself to relive the horrific shooting. He explains how the technique works: "It switches your recollection of the events from the right side of the brain to the left so it's no longer attached with your emotions." He adds: "That made all the difference in the world for me."[53]

Drug Treatment

Along with the various therapy methods used to treat mental illness, young people may also be treated with prescription medications. Teens with depression, for instance, are often prescribed antidepressants, and some of these medications are also effective at treating anxiety disorders. The drugs are controversial, however, and physicians have been accused of prescribing them too readily or not monitoring patient progress closely enough. According to Florida psychiatrist R. Scott Benson, youth depression is a serious problem, and antidepressants can be an essential part of treatment. But he also says that physicians should not just hand out a prescription and consider that the solution to the young person's problem. "Whatever therapy or medication we prescribe," says Benson, "we need to have a clearly developed treatment plan, and make sure that we are seeing them progress as we expect them to."[54]

Antidepressants are controversial because of a possible link to suicidal thoughts in young patients. In 2004 a study by the US Food and Drug Administration (FDA) found that suicidal thinking or suicidal behavior doubled among patients younger than age eighteen if they were taking antidepressants. The FDA then issued its strictest guideline, known as the black box warning, for the use of antidepressants in treating teen mental illness. Only one drug (fluoxetine, or Prozac) is approved by the FDA for children and teens suffering from major depression, although doctors can prescribe other drugs as they see fit.

It is a common practice among mental health professionals to treat patients with one or more types of therapy combined with prescription medications. And according to a study published in September 2017, this sort of treatment is extremely effective for young people suffering from severe anxiety. The study involved nearly five hundred youth aged seven to seventeen. One group participated in CBT only, youths in a second group were given an antidepressant called sertraline (brand name Zoloft), and members of a third group were treated with both. After twelve weeks, 63 percent of the youth who were treated with both CBT and sertraline were free from anxiety. This was in sharp contrast to the youth who were treated with either CBT or sertraline, rather than the combination. Among that group, 25 percent to 30 percent were anxiety-free after twelve weeks.

The researchers cannot say for sure why the combination treatment works so much better than drugs or CBT alone. One theory is that the medication helps ease anxiety enough that

> "Whatever therapy or medication we prescribe, we need to have a clearly developed treatment plan, and make sure that we are seeing [patients] progress as we expect them to."[54]
>
> —R. Scott Benson, a psychiatrist from Pensacola, Florida

Hope for Severe Depression Sufferers

For many young people with mental illness, a combination of therapy and medication often helps relieve symptoms and keep the illness in check. But for some teens, like Ben Finder, that does not help. Finder was an athletic thirteen-year-old middle schooler when a dark cloud of depression seemed to come out of nowhere. He said nothing to his parents at first, but after a few months of being consumed with thoughts of suicide, he finally told them. He tried every conceivable treatment, from a variety of medications to different kinds of therapy, and also spent time in a psychiatric hospital. He was diagnosed with "treatment-refractory" depression, a form of depression that does not respond to the usual treatments. Hearing this, he began to feel that his situation was hopeless.

Then his father, a doctor, heard about an experimental treatment for people with a deficiency in folate. One of the B vitamins, folate is needed by the body for healthy cell division and growth, as well as normal brain and nerve functioning. Finder was tested, and results showed that he had a folate deficiency. He was immediately started on high doses of folinic acid (a form of folic acid) to replenish folate in his body. The results were nothing short of miraculous. Within a month Finder felt better than he had in a long time. As of August 2016 he was a happy, healthy high school junior who was looking forward to college and planning what his major would be.

young people can benefit more from therapy sessions. "Meds reduce the level of anxiety, we do know that," says psychiatrist Jerome Taylor, who was lead author of the study. "It's possible that helps [the patients] engage more in the therapy where they couldn't before."[55]

When More Care Is Needed

Yet even a combination of drugs and therapy is not always enough. Some teens struggling with mental illness need more intensive treatment than they can get through outpatient therapy. When a health care provider makes that decision, the young person is admitted to a psychiatric hospital or residential treatment facility. This was the situation with a young man named Jake from

North Carolina, who suffered from such crippling anxiety that he attempted suicide more than once. Jake's physicians determined that residential treatment was best for him, and he was sent to the Mountain Valley residential treatment facility in New Hampshire.

During his stay at the facility, Jake engaged in different types of therapy, including exposure therapy, which helped him get over his greatest fear: being a failure at life. So great was his fear of failure that he tended to lapse into catastrophizing. For instance, if he failed a single quiz in high school, he would think, "then I'll get a bad grade in the class, I won't get into the college I want, I

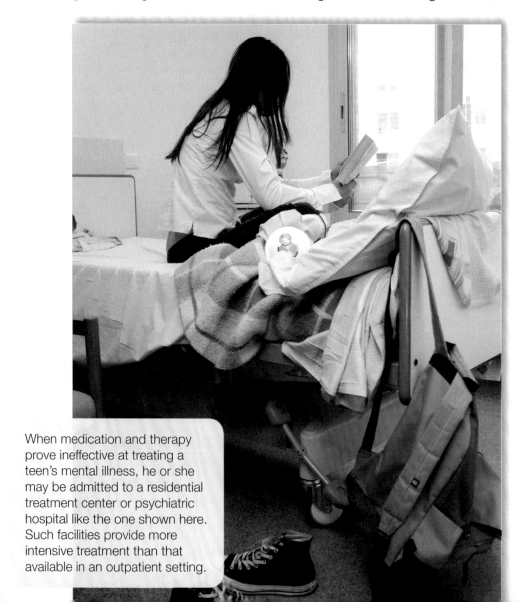

When medication and therapy prove ineffective at treating a teen's mental illness, he or she may be admitted to a residential treatment center or psychiatric hospital like the one shown here. Such facilities provide more intensive treatment than that available in an outpatient setting.

won't get a good job and I'll be a total failure."[56] Through exposure therapy, Jake learned not to blow fears out of proportion and to manage his anxiety, rather than letting it control him.

Hospitalization is often necessary for teens with anorexia because the self-starvation that is characteristic of the illness can be deadly. When young people starve themselves, they are not just getting thinner; they are starving their vital organs of essential nutrients. The result can be catastrophic, leading to heart attack and the shutting down of other organs. This almost happened to Tanner Tangen after he developed anorexia and starved off 40 pounds (18.1 kg). At only fourteen years old, Tangen was warned by doctors that he could have a heart attack at any time. He was admitted to the hospital, and doctors said his was one of the worst cases they had ever seen. "I was going to die," says Tangen. "I was so weak, so frail and bony."[57]

While hospitalized, Tangen was put on a rigid schedule consisting of mealtimes, school, therapy, and free time. He was monitored by hospital staff constantly, and his weight gain was watched carefully. Through therapy, he gradually became comfortable with eating again. After being discharged from the hospital, Tangen wanted to reach out to other young people who suffer from eating disorders. He began recording anorexia talks and posting them to YouTube. "I'm trying to help people,"[58] he says.

A Troubling Reality

Even though there are a variety of treatment options for young people with mental illness, most of these youths are never treated. According to a 2015 Child Mind Institute report, 80 percent of youth with anxiety disorders get no treatment, and the same is true of 60 percent of youth with depression. On average, only about one-third of young people with mental illness ever get the help they need. Without treatment, symptoms typically worsen—and schoolwork, motivation, state of mind, and relationships with family and friends often suffer.

The most disturbing result of not getting treatment is heightened risk of suicide. According to the Centers for Disease Control and Prevention, suicide is the second leading cause of death among teens aged fifteen to nineteen. Young people who suffer from mental illness and do not receive treatment are more likely to think of death as their only option.

There are a number of reasons why so many young people do not get the treatment they need. One is that they are often too ashamed or scared to ask for help, or they do not know whom to turn to for help. Another huge barrier to treatment is the exorbitant cost of health care. The residential facility where Jake stayed cost $910 per day—more than $80,000 for three months. Even attending outpatient therapy sessions can be cost-prohibitive for young people whose families are struggling financially, especially if they do not have health insurance.

One of the most troubling reasons most youth are not treated for mental illness is a severe shortage of mental health professionals who specialize in children and teens. According to the American Academy of Child and Adolescent Psychiatry, there is one child psychiatrist for every eighteen hundred youth who need treatment for mental health issues. "No barrier may be more alarming than the scarcity of providers,"[59] says Rob Haskell.

A Pressing Need

Alarming numbers of young people suffer from depression, anxiety, and other mental illnesses. As these numbers have continued to soar in recent years, experts have begun to refer to a mental illness epidemic among youth and call it a crisis situation. The good news is that many excellent treatment options are available, including a variety of therapies and prescription medications. Sadly, however, only a fraction of young people who need these treatments ever have access to them. Mental health advocates would like very much to see that change in the coming years.

Chapter 4

What Is It Like to Live with Mental Illness?

When Benjamin Shapiro was caught in the throes of OCD, he often wondered whether he would ever feel normal again. He had become so dependent on the rituals he performed, and so consumed with his obsessive fears, that he could not imagine being free of them. When Shapiro's illness reached the point of being unbearable, his parents sought intensive treatment for him. Although it was not an easy path to travel, he slowly but steadily began making progress. Now a college student, Shapiro feels like a typical young man—"a luxury my family was not sure I'd ever have," he says. "The normalcy of friends, classes, sports, acting in a play, even traveling abroad on my own, feels like a battle won."[60]

Because of what he went through and all that he has learned, Shapiro has become a vocal advocate for young people who struggle with mental illness. Before he was treated for OCD, he felt different from all the other kids his age, convinced that no one could possibly relate to his struggles. "OCD made me feel alienated in a world I was sure only I understood," he says. "Had I realized how false that was, that there are millions of us out there, I might have felt a little less alone." One of his volunteer activities was being a mentor at a day camp for kids with mental illness. "I was able to tell the young campers that I'd been where they are, that I know what it feels like to be trapped in your own head," he says. "And that, while there may be no cure, there is hope."[61]

The Courage to Reach Out

It is common for young people who develop mental illness to be confused about what is happening to them. Many, like Shapiro, feel alienated from their classmates and friends. This was true of a high school girl from Palo Alto, California, who writes anonymously about her difficult struggle with depression and an anxiety disorder. She was stricken with panic attacks at age twelve, and before long, she was overwhelmed by sadness that would not go away. Immediately, she began to feel like an outsider who was no longer like the other teens she had known. "I heard a voice in my head telling me I was different from my peers," she says. "I told myself the voice would silence itself in time, and yet it only grew louder."[62]

The girl visited a therapist who suggested she take antidepressants, but she chose not to. Instead, she opted to try getting better on her own by trying to distract herself from negative feelings. That, however, did not work, as she explains: "Although I was surrounded by people, no words can begin to express the loneliness I felt. Even in a roomful of people, I felt sheltered and insecure. I constantly told myself that I was unwanted—unwanted in this social situation, but even more importantly, unwanted on this earth." When she was a junior in high school, the girl finally had to admit that she was getting worse, not better, and needed help. She started getting therapy and taking antidepressants, and this made a huge difference in how she felt. "I have finally come to terms with the fact that it will take time and patience to improve my state," she says, "but it's better than giving up altogether."[63]

Young people who suffer from depression may feel alone and unwanted. Sometimes being in a group with others who are also affected by depression can combat feelings of isolation.

Although she has written about her painful battle with anxiety and depression, the girl chooses to remain anonymous. This is not because she is ashamed, but rather because of the widespread lack of understanding of mental illness and the stigma attached to it. "Throughout my life," she says, "when I have chosen to share the truth about my depression and anxiety with others, the most common reaction I've received is, 'Wow, you don't seem like it.'"[64] To avoid such an uncomfortable, embarrassing situation, she has learned that it is best to hide any signs of her mental illness from other people. She writes:

It has taken me years to master the masking of my symptoms, and at this point I'm an expert in this craft. I am positive I am not the only one who has felt obligated to mask what is going on behind closed doors, and because of this, I hope to encourage a community where my peers feel open to unmasking themselves. After all, no one deserves to feel as if they need to hide the truth about themselves.[65]

Fighting the Stigma

One of the girl's passions is to help educate people about mental illness. She wants people to realize that it is common, it affects young people as well as adults, and no one chooses to have depression, anxiety, or any other mental illness. "While we aren't in control of the spread of these illnesses," she says, "we are in control of how we approach them. If we can create an environment in which those around us feel open to sharing their disorder, we're one step closer to a fast recovery for those individuals like me."[66]

Research has shown that there is a widespread lack of understanding and numerous misconceptions about mental illness. This is known as a stigma, which refers to the stereotypes, negativity, and prejudice that result from misconceptions about mental health conditions and the people who suffer from them. The Mayo Clinic explains:

> Unfortunately, negative attitudes and beliefs toward people who have a mental health condition are common. Stigma can lead to discrimination. Discrimination may be obvious and direct, such as someone making a negative remark about your mental illness or your treatment. Or it may be unintentional or subtle, such as someone avoiding you because the person assumes you could be unstable, violent or dangerous due to your mental illness.[67]

Because of all the misconceptions about mental illness, researchers are interested in hearing about young people's personal experiences, thoughts, and beliefs. In April 2017 the health and wellness organization HealthCorps surveyed nearly four hundred high school students. One question was about whether they had ever experienced feelings of overwhelming sadness, and 76 percent said they had. Of those, 45 percent of the teens said they often felt sad for no reason. When asked whether they sometimes felt worthless, more than 50 percent said yes.

Only Darkness

Some teens find living with mental illness to be too painful to bear. Either they have not been treated or treatment has not helped them—and tragically, they would rather die than continue living in constant emotional pain. According to NAMI, depression and other mental illnesses are strong risk factors for suicide. At least 90 percent of people who take their own lives suffer from some kind of mental illness.

This was the case with Will Trautwein, who was a freshman in high school when he committed suicide in 2010. His parents had no idea that their son was suffering from depression. He was popular and always seemed upbeat and well adjusted. He was an athlete and a musician who was from a happy home. His family and friends were devastated by his death, and they wish that he had reached out for help. In his memory, and to help prevent the same tragedy among other teens, his parents founded the Will to Live Foundation. It is run by teens who organize events, raise funds, and help each other through depression and mental illness. "It's very healing for us to be able to turn something so bad into something so good," says Will's father, John Trautwein.

Quoted in Joe Parker, "Will to Live Foundation Gets Teens Talking About Mental Illness, Depression," *North Fulton Herald*, March 29, 2017. www.northfulton.com.

The researchers also asked the teens to share their opinions about depression, and 68 percent said they believed it was a real illness—but the remaining 32 percent thought it was a weakness that people needed to work on. This was troubling to HealthCorps researchers, because it showed at least one serious misconception about depression among teens. "The results of our poll make me wonder how many students who struggle with their mental health are afraid to reach out for help due to the stigma attached to mental illnesses," says research scientist Jean Lim. "It is heartbreaking to hear that 56% of students feel worthless at times."[68]

Communicating Through Art

One of the most stigmatized mental illnesses is schizophrenia, and this is hurtful for young people who suffer from it. It is still a common belief, for instance, that people with schizophrenia have multiple personalities, which is not true. Another widespread myth is that schizophrenia sufferers are violent or dangerous, but neither can be backed up with definitive evidence.

"This stigma still represents a major obstacle to many people in terms of identifying signs of illness in a timely manner and seeking appropriate treatment," says physician John Kane. Along with being a schizophrenia specialist, Kane is also a mental health policy advocate who works on behalf of people who have the mental illness. "We are engaged in a variety of attempts to reduce stigma through better public education, particularly among young people,"[69] he says.

Kate Fenner, a young woman from Los Angeles, California, was diagnosed with schizophrenia when she was seventeen. Like

Some people cope with their mental illness by expressing what they are feeling in works of art. This painting was created by a person diagnosed with schizophrenia.

others with the illness, Fenner suffers from psychosis, which involves hallucinations that are often disturbing and frightening. "The hallucinations give me anxiety and a sense of malice," she says, adding that they happen on a regular basis. "Auditory hallucinations are an everyday occurrence, so it's a constant stream of noise."[70] She also has tactile hallucinations, during which she sees and feels spiders and bugs crawling on her skin and biting her.

> "The hallucinations give me anxiety and a sense of malice."[70]
>
> —Kate Fenner, a young woman who suffers from schizophrenia

As frightening as these hallucinations are, Fenner has found a way to channel her fears—through art. "I started drawing my hallucinations when I felt trapped and suffocated by them," she says. "It often feels like everything is fake, and the world around me is a big conspiracy. So drawing started to become comforting." Fenner's drawings are haunting, depicting what she sees, feels, and hears because of psychosis. She uploads them to her Instagram account and shares them with thousands of followers. Although this can be intimidating because some people say cruel and hurtful things, she does not let that stop her. "I'm not bothered by any negative comments," she says. "If I can live through schizophrenia I can handle someone's harsh opinion."[71]

Fenner says that overall, people she meets online have been very kind. Many say she inspires them, which especially pleases her. Along with using the drawings as a way of coping with psychosis, she wants her artwork to raise awareness of mental illness. It is her goal to help others who are struggling know that they matter and are not alone, as she explains: "I'm being open about this in the hopes that someone will come across it and not feel alone in their pain and struggle, and they get a sense of hope."[72]

A Plea for Understanding

Many young people struggling with mental illness feel alone and isolated. Although everyone's experience is different, and no two patients are exactly the same, a common thread among them is their desire and need to be understood and accepted for who they are. When considering mental illness, people, in general, tend to be more judgmental than compassionate—and that can be difficult for young people who suffer from schizophrenia, depression, crippling anxiety, or other mental illnesses.

Hannah Hilgeman knows this struggle well. The Columbus, Ohio, teen has panic attacks several times a day, with no predictable trigger. "It's like a light switch," she says. "One moment everything is amazing. . . . I trust the future, whatever it may hold. In this moment I am content. Switch! All of a sudden, fear. The laughter that just filled my ears disperses." Hilgeman goes to therapy and takes medications but still suffers from panic disorder as well as depression. "I am completely and utterly at the mercy of this horrendous monster," she says. "It can steal my state of total content and replace it with a panicked soul, gearing up to fight."[73]

> "I am completely and utterly at the mercy of this horrendous monster."[73]
>
> —Hannah Hilgeman, a young woman who suffers from panic attacks and depression

Hilgeman is aware that when she is in the midst of a panic attack, she can seem like a totally different person to those around her. As much as she understands why this could frustrate them, what happens is not within her control. "If only they knew," she says. "If only they knew the lack of control I possess during my anxiety episodes, the constant feeling of fear and feeling as if death himself is breathing right on my neck." Hilgeman's wish is that people would try harder to understand, rather than calling her crazy and making snide comments like "Just get some help and get over it," which someone said to her. She encourages people to show kindness toward those with mental illness and try their best to be understanding, even though they may not understand at all. "Have compassion," she says. "See it from their point of view."[74]

Fighting for Awareness

In 2014 two teenage girls from Ann Arbor, Michigan, learned by accident that they both had depression. Madeline Halpert and Eva Rosenfeld were editors of their high school newspaper and had traveled to a journalism conference. One noticed a bottle of the antidepressant Prozac in the other's bag and remarked that she also took the drug. For the first time, they opened up to each other about depression and how they were coping with it. They decided to do more with that knowledge than keep it only between them. To help fight the stigma of mental illness, the girls proposed devoting an issue of their school newspaper to the personal stories of teens who were suffering from mental illness.

The girls interviewed a number of teens who candidly shared their own battles with depression, eating disorders, anxiety, and other mental illnesses. For many, it was the first time they had revealed these struggles. Parents signed consent forms for all teens whose stories would be featured. But their stories were never printed. As the students were putting the information together, they were told that the project had been pulled; school administrators forbade them to go forward with it. Halpert and Rosenfeld were terribly disappointed, as they write in a *New York Times* article: "By interviewing these teenagers for our newspaper, we tried—and failed—to start small in the fight against stigma. Unfortunately, we've learned this won't be easy. It seems that those who are charged with advocating for our well-being aren't ready yet to let us have an open and honest dialogue about depression."

Madeline Halpert and Eva Rosenfeld, "Depressed, but Not Ashamed," *New York Times*, May 22, 2014. www.nytimes.com.

Desperate to Cope

Some young people become so emotionally overwrought from the effects of mental illness that they turn to dysfunctional, harmful methods of coping, such as self-injury. This was true of Faith-Ann Bishop, who first started cutting herself when she was in the eighth grade. At the time she was consumed by anxiety and could not seem to escape from it. It affected her ability to sleep, made her physically ill, and often kept her home from school. Late one night, desperate to find relief from the anxiety, Bishop sat on the edge of the bathtub holding a metal clip from a pen in her hand. She sliced into the soft skin of her abdomen, and blood oozed out of the cut. Yet despite the sharp pain, she felt a sense of relief from the emotional turmoil that was plaguing her.

That was the beginning of repetitive self-injury for Bishop, who continued to cut herself for three years. "For a while I didn't want to stop, because it was my only coping mechanism," she says. "I hadn't learned any other way."[75] Like most young people who engage in self-harm, she had no intention of committing suicide. Rather, she was trying to substitute physical pain for the psychological pain caused by her anxiety and depression.

Bishop was careful to cut in places that were not visible to others, such as her arms and torso. When her mother discovered what she had been doing, Bishop was a junior in high school. Without thinking, she had cut herself on the wrist where it was visible to her mom. "I lifted my arm to move my hair, and she saw it," says Bishop. Her mom remained calm and asked Bishop if she was cutting herself, and Bishop replied: "Yes, I am cutting, and I want to stop."[76] Soon afterward, Bishop and her parents started family therapy, and Bishop was on the path to recovery. Once she started treatment, her urge to self-injure began to diminish.

Bishop is realistic about her mental illness. She believes that to some extent she will always struggle with depression and anxiety. "It's a condition that's not going to totally disappear from my life," she says. But she now believes that she has the tools to cope with mental illness in a healthy way. One of the best things she did for herself was to channel her feelings and emotions into a creative project. She joined a teen program in Maine called Project Aware. As part of the group, Bishop wrote and directed a short film about anxiety and depression in teens called *The Road Back*. "I had a place where I could be open and talk about my life and the issues I was having," she says, "and then I could project them in an artistic way."[77] Today Bishop attends film school in Los Angeles, California, and she looks forward to a career writing and producing movies.

Learning to Live Again

Envisioning a happy future can be very difficult for young people who are fighting to recover from mental illness. Often, even after going through treatment, it takes all their energy just to make it from one day to the next. "Things get easier," says nineteen-year-old Maris Degener. "They do. But it's like a cancer—it can hide, it can seem to disappear, but it's never really gone. It's a lifelong remission that leaves you and everyone around second-guessing all the time." When she was a freshman in high school, Degener suffered from anorexia and was hospitalized for three weeks. Although she was in danger of dying and hospitalization was her only hope, she still "screamed and cried the whole way there."[78]

Degener found hospitalization to be the most miserable experience of her life. After starving herself for so long, being forced to eat felt like torture. "But the one thing that place did," she says,

Living with mental illness requires identifying successful coping strategies. For many, physical activity such as yoga is an effective tool that helps them mentally as well as physically.

"was keep me from ever wanting to go back." After being released, Degener could focus on nothing but getting better physically. "For a while, that was my only motivation—to get better," she says. "My mind was sick, but I knew that the only thing that would keep me out of a wheelchair was getting my body stable and bringing it back from the brink."[79]

> "I'm meant to live, and I finally know what that means."[81]
>
> —Maris Degener, a young woman who recovered from anorexia with the help of yoga

Degener returned to school and tried to get back to living her normal life. But even though her body had healed, her mind was not yet healed. "People think that therapy and a hospital stay . . . will send you sprinting into recovery," she says, "but for so many it's just not true." Then, toward the end of her sophomore year, Degener discovered something that changed her life in ways she could never have imagined: yoga. She loved it from her very first practice, as she writes:

I fell in love with the way movement felt in my body, the contraction of musculature, the breath circulating through my veins. I felt like a foot that'd been asleep too long slowly regaining feeling, slipping into a world that was almost overwhelming with sensation and experience. I suddenly wanted nothing more than to feel what feeling alive felt like—to see if I could find that person I thought had died inside of me long before I got to know her.[80]

Degener's passion for yoga grew stronger as time went by, and she credits it for the mental healing that she had so desperately craved. She went through instructor training, and today she teaches yoga to others. "I found who I am and who I want to be," she says. "I found the thing I want to stick around and be strong for." Along with teaching yoga, Degener is also in college and writes articles about her personal journey of mental illness and recovery. "I'm meant to live," she says, "and I finally know what that means."[81]

Never Give Up

Degener fought hard to get to where she is today, and she is the first to say that living with mental illness is not easy. It takes work. It takes determination. It takes resilience. And it takes motivation. Treatment can make a positive difference, but it is not a cure. "You'll try again, and again, and again," she says. "You'll slip up, you'll relapse, you'll feel like a failure. But somewhere along the line, you find something, just one little thing, that makes getting back up again feel worth it."[82] For Degener, that was yoga and a passion for teaching. For Kate Fenner, it is being able to put her haunting thoughts into drawings that might help young people who are also suffering. Other teens have their own ways of coping with their illnesses. Perhaps the most important thing for these young people to remember is that there is always hope.

Source Notes

Introduction: Disorders of the Mind

1. Benjamin Shapiro, "OCD Is No Longer in Charge: One Kid's Story," *The Guest Room* (blog), *Psychology Today*, May 6, 2014. www.psychologytoday.com.
2. Shapiro, "OCD Is No Longer in Charge."
3. Joseph M. Rey et al., "History of Child Psychiatry," in *IACAPAP Textbook of Child and Adolescent Mental Health*, 2015. http://iacapap.org.
4. Rey et al., "History of Child Psychiatry."
5. National Institute of Mental Health, "The Teen Brain: 6 Things to Know," 2016. www.nimh.nih.gov.
6. American Psychiatric Association, "What Is Mental Illness?," 2015. www.psychiatry.org.

Chapter 1: What Is Mental Illness?

7. Rob Haskell, "Why Is Anxiety So Common Among the Young?," *Vogue*, November 1, 2016. www.vogue.com.
8. Haskell, "Why Is Anxiety So Common Among the Young?"
9. Quoted in Judith Orozco, "Teens Anxiety—a Hidden, Lonely Struggle," *San Jose (CA) Mercury News*, June 8, 2017. www.mercurynews.com.
10. Sara Kidman, "The Hurdles of Being a 21-Year-Old with Generalized Anxiety Disorder," *The Mighty* (blog), March 25, 2017. https://themighty.com.

11. Stefan G. Hofmann, interviewed by Olga Khazan, "What Is Social Anxiety?," *Atlantic*, October 22, 2015. www.theatlantic .com.

12. Natasha Daniels, "What to Do When Your Child Is Having a Panic Attack," *Parenting Anxious Kids* (blog), Psych Central, September 2016. https://blogs.psychcentral.com.

13. Hannah Hilgeman, "How My Anxiety Is Like a Light Switch," *The Mighty* (blog), May 1, 2017. https://themighty.com.

14. Anxiety and Depression Association of America, "Depression," 2013. https://adaa.org.

15. Jeneisha Janice, "10 Embarrassing Things About Being a Teenager with Anxiety," *The Mighty* (blog), May 25, 2017. https://themighty.com.

16. Quoted in Lisa Esposito, "How Depression and Anxiety Go Hand-in-Hand," *U.S. News & World Report*, March 10, 2017. https://health.usnews.com.

17. Alisha Gregg, "When OCD Means Living in a World of 'What Ifs,'" *The Mighty* (blog), July 5, 2016. https://themighty.com.

18. Naomi Moresi, "Hidden PTSD in Teenagers," *Huffington Post*, May 9, 2017. www.huffingtonpost.com.

19. Moresi, "Hidden PTSD in Teenagers."

20. Quoted in Kirsten Weir, "New Insights on Eating Disorders," *Monitor on Psychology*, April 2016. www.apa.org.

21. Celine Sauve, "What I Wish Others Understood About My Bulimia," *The Mighty* (blog), June 8, 2017. https://themighty .com.

Chapter 2: What Causes Mental Illness?

22. Quoted in Markham Heid, "We Need to Talk About Kids and Smartphones," *Time*, October 10, 2017. http://time.com.

23. Jesse Singal, "What Is the Connection Between Personality and Mental Illness?," *Science of Us* (blog), *New York*, May 26, 2017. http://nymag.com.

24. National Alliance on Mental Illness, "Mental Health Conditions," 2017. www.nami.org.

25. Diane McIntosh, "What Causes Mental Illness? It's Complicated," *The Blog*, *Huffington Post*, March 22, 2017. www.huffingtonpost.ca.

26. Quoted in Karen Weintraub, "Schizophrenia Has Clear Genetic Ties, New Study Finds," *USA Today*, July 21, 2014. www.usatoday.com.

27. Saul McLeod, "Nature vs. Nurture in Psychology," Simply Psychology, 2007. www.simplypsychology.org.

28. Haskell, "Why Is Anxiety So Common Among the Young?"

29. Maia Szalavitz, "How Child Abuse Primes the Brain for Future Mental Illness," *Time*, February 15, 2012. http://healthland.time.com.

30. Martin H. Teicher et al., "Childhood Maltreatment Is Associated with Reduced Volume in the Hippocampal Subfields CA3, Dentate Gyrus, and Subiculum," *PNAS*, February 28, 2012. www.pnas.org.

31. Weill Cornell Medicine, "New Studies Illuminate Brain's Complex Neurotransmission Machinery, Point to Potential Source of Problems Leading to Neurodegenerative and Psychiatric Conditions," June 22, 2011. https://news.weill.cornell.edu.

32. Quoted in Christopher Bergland, "Why Is the Teen Brain So Vulnerable?," *The Athlete's Way* (blog), *Psychology Today*, December 19, 2013. www.psychologytoday.com.

33. Quoted in Weir, "New Insights on Eating Disorders."

34. Quoted in Chloe Melas, "Zayn Malik Reveals Eating Disorder Battle While in One Direction," CNN, November 1, 2016. www.cnn.com.

35. Ron J. Steingard, "Mood Disorders and Teenage Girls," Child Mind Institute, 2017. https://childmind.org.

36. Quoted in Patti Neighmond, "Depression Strikes Today's Teen Girls Especially Hard," NPR, February 13, 2017. www.npr.org.

37. Quoted in Stanford Medicine, "Traumatic Stress Changes Brains of Boys, Girls Differently," news release, November 11, 2016. https://med.stanford.edu.

38. Quoted in Stanford Medicine, "Traumatic Stress Changes Brains of Boys, Girls Differently."
39. Quoted in Benoit Denizet-Lewis, "Why Are More American Teenagers than Ever Suffering from Severe Anxiety?," *New York Times Magazine*, October 11, 2017. www.nytimes.com.
40. Quoted in Denizet-Lewis, "Why Are More American Teenagers than Ever Suffering from Severe Anxiety?"
41. Quoted in Susanna Schrobsdorff, "Teen Depression and Anxiety: Why the Kids Are Not Alright," *Time*, November 7, 2016. http://time.com.
42. Quoted in Schrobsdorff, "Teen Depression and Anxiety."
43. Quoted in Denizet-Lewis, "Why Are More American Teenagers than Ever Suffering from Severe Anxiety?"

Chapter 3: Can Mental Illness Be Treated or Cured?

44. Quoted in Jacki Ochoa, "#BreakingSilence: Helping Kids and Teens Identify Mental Illness," 23ABC News, February 9, 2017. www.turnto23.com.
45. Association for Children's Mental Health, "Children's Mental Health Treatment and Support," 2017. www.acmh-mi.org.
46. Adam Husney, "Family Therapy," WebMD, November 20, 2015. www.webmd.com.
47. Quoted in Juliana Bunim, "Teens with Bulimia Recover Faster When Parents Are Included in Treatment," UCSF, September 17, 2015. www.ucsf.edu.
48. National Alliance on Mental Illness, "Psychotherapy," 2017. www.nami.org.
49. Haskell, "Why Is Anxiety So Common Among the Young?"
50. Quoted in Denizet-Lewis, "Why Are More American Teenagers than Ever Suffering from Severe Anxiety?"
51. Quoted in Lindsey Tanner, "Making Raped Teens Relive Trauma Works, Study Says," *San Diego Union-Tribune*, December 24, 2013. www.sandiegouniontribune.com.

52. Quoted in Tanner, "Making Raped Teens Relive Trauma Works, Study Says."

53. Quoted in Tony Boone, "UNO's Kyler Erickson Is Well-Versed in Comebacks," *Mavericks Today*, January 13, 2016. www.omaha.com.

54. Quoted in Alice Park, "Teen Depression Treatment Is an Increasingly Thorny Issue," *Time*, June 8, 2016. http://time.com.

55. Quoted in Angus Chen, "For Children with Severe Anxiety, Drugs Plus Therapy Help Best," NPR, October 2, 2017. www.npr.org.

56. Quoted in Denizet-Lewis, "Why Are More American Teenagers than Ever Suffering from Severe Anxiety?"

57. Holly Hudson, "Tanner's Tribulations: A Young Man's Battle with Anorexia Nervosa," *Waterloo-Cedar Falls (IA) Courier*, October 9, 2016. http://wcfcourier.com.

58. Quoted in Hudson, "Tanner's Tribulations."

59. Haskell, "Why Is Anxiety So Common Among the Young?"

Chapter 4: What Is It Like to Live with Mental Illness?

60. Shapiro, "OCD Is No Longer in Charge."

61. Shapiro, "OCD Is No Longer in Charge."

62. Palo Alto High School student, "Guest Opinion: Unmasking the Truth—Beyond the Stigma of Mental Illness," Palo Alto Online, March 22, 2016. https://paloaltoonline.com.

63. Palo Alto High School student, "Guest Opinion."

64. Palo Alto High School student, "Guest Opinion."

65. Palo Alto High School student, "Guest Opinion."

66. Palo Alto High School student, "Guest Opinion."

67. Mayo Clinic, "Mental Health: Overcoming the Stigma of Mental Illness," May 24, 2017. www.mayoclinic.org.

68. Quoted in Javad Ali, "Majority of Teens Have Experienced Signs of Depression, Feel Worthless at Times New Poll Says," HealthCorps, May 24, 2017. www.healthcorps.org/april-depression-poll-2017.

69. Quoted in Tammy Scileppi, "John Kane: Doctor Battles Stigma of Mental Illness," *TimesLedger* (Queens, NY), May 27, 2016. www.timesledger.com.

70. Quoted in Hattie Gladwell, "Teen Depicts Living with Schizophrenia Through Truly Haunting Drawings," Metro, April 24, 2017. http://metro.co.uk.

71. Quoted in Gladwell, "Teen Depicts Living with Schizophrenia Through Truly Haunting Drawings."

72. Quoted in Gladwell, "Teen Depicts Living with Schizophrenia Through Truly Haunting Drawings."

73. Hilgeman, "How My Anxiety Is like a Light Switch."

74. Hilgeman, "How My Anxiety Is like a Light Switch."

75. Quoted in Schrobsdorff, "Teen Depression and Anxiety."

76. Quoted in Schrobsdorff, "Teen Depression and Anxiety."

77. Quoted in Schrobsdorff, "Teen Depression and Anxiety."

78. Maris Degener, "Yoga Saved My Life, Now I Teach It," CNN iReport, August 14, 2015. http://ireport.cnn.com.

79. Degener, "Yoga Saved My Life, Now I Teach It."

80. Degener, "Yoga Saved My Life, Now I Teach It."

81. Degener, "Yoga Saved My Life, Now I Teach It."

82. Degener, "Yoga Saved My Life, Now I Teach It."

Organizations and Websites

American Psychiatric Association

1000 Wilson Blvd., Suite 1825
Arlington, VA 22209
website: www.psychiatry.org

The American Psychiatric Association represents more than thirty-seven thousand members who are involved in psychiatric practice, research, and academia. Numerous articles and publications about youth mental illness are available through the website's search engine.

American Psychological Association (APA)

750 First St. NE
Washington, DC 20002
website: www.apa.org

The APA is the largest scientific and professional organization that represents the field of psychology in the United States. Its website links to newspaper articles, research data, and a number of online publications that focus on mental illness and its effects on young people.

Anxiety and Depression Association of America (ADAA)

8701 Georgia Ave., Suite 412
Silver Spring, MD 20910
website: www.adaa.org

Through education and research, the ADAA is dedicated to the prevention, treatment, and cure of anxiety, depressive, obsessive-compulsive, and trauma-related disorders. Its website offers

70

numerous publications, along with webinars, an online support group, an e-newsletter, and links to a number of blogs.

Mayo Clinic
200 First St. SW
Rochester, MN 55905
website: www.mayoclinic.org

The Mayo Clinic is the world's largest nonprofit medical group practice. Its website includes links to a great deal of information about mental illness, including in young people.

Mental Health America
2000 N. Beauregard St., 6th Floor
Alexandria, VA 22311
website: www.mentalhealthamerica.net

Formed in 1909, Mental Health America is the nation's oldest advocacy organization that addresses mental health. Its website contains numerous resources related to mental illness.

Minding Your Mind (MYM)
42 W. Lancaster Ave., 2nd Floor
Ardmore, PA 19003
website: http://mindingyourmind.org

MYM provides mental health education to children, teens, young adults, and their parents, teachers, and school administrators. Its website offers a variety of publications related to mental illness, many of which are specifically for young people.

National Alliance on Mental Illness (NAMI)
3803 N. Fairfax Dr., Suite 100
Arlington, VA 22203
website: www.nami.org

NAMI is a nonprofit advocacy group for families and people affected by mental illness in the United States. The NAMI website links to its Child & Adolescent Action Center, which works to improve the lives of children, teens, and young adults affected by mental illness. Both sites provide a variety of resources about mental illness in young people.

National Child Traumatic Stress Network (NCTSN)

NCCTS—Duke University
411 W. Chapel Hill St., Suite 200
Durham, NC 27701
website: www.nctsn.org

The NCTSN works to improve access to care, treatment, and services for children and teens exposed to traumatic events. Its website contains a multitude of resources, including information about traumatic stress, an e-bulletin, news, research, articles, and links for more information.

National Eating Disorders Association (NEDA)

200 W. Forty-First St., Suite 1203
New York, NY 10036
website: www.nationaleatingdisorders.org

NEDA works to prevent eating disorders and provides treatment referrals to those suffering from them. Its website offers a variety of publications about eating disorders, resources for eating disorder sufferers and families, research papers, and a link to the NEDA blog.

National Institute of Mental Health (NIMH)

6001 Executive Blvd., Room 6200, MSC 9663
Bethesda, MD 20892
website: www.nimh.nih.gov

An agency of the US Department of Health and Human Services, the NIMH is the largest research organization in the world specializing in mental illness. The NIMH website's Child and Adolescent Mental Health section contains news, studies, publications for children and teens, information on treatment options, and links for more information.

For Further Research

Books

Shari Bradi, *It's Not What You're Eating, It's What's Eating You*. New York: Skyhorse, 2018.

Jessica Burkhart, *Life Inside My Mind: 31 Authors Share Their Personal Struggles*. New York: Simon & Schuster, 2018.

Sue Knowles et al., *My Anxiety Handbook: Getting Back on Track*. Philadelphia: Jessica Kingsley, 2018.

Raychelle Cassada Lohmann and Sheela Raja, *The Sexual Trauma Workbook for Teen Girls: A Guide to Recovery from Sexual Assault and Abuse*. Oakland, CA: New Harbinger, 2016.

Peggy J. Parks, *Teen Depression*. Farmington Hills, MI: Lucent, 2013.

Peggy J. Parks, *Teens and Stress*. San Diego, CA: ReferencePoint, 2015.

Sheela Raja and Jaya Ashrafi, *The PTSD Survival Guide for Teens*. Oakland, CA: New Harbinger, 2018.

Internet Sources

Kate Fenner, "I Was Diagnosed with Schizophrenia at the Age of 17, So I Started Drawing My Hallucinations to Cope with It," Bored Panda, April 2017. www.boredpanda.com/18-year-old -schizophrenic-artist-drawing-hallucinations.

Jacqueline Howard, "Why Teen Mental Health Experts Are Focused on '13 Reasons Why,'" CNN, April 25, 2017. www.cnn.com/2017/04/25/health/13-reasons-why-teen-suicide-debate-explainer/index.html.

Jacki Ochoa, "#BreakingSilence: Local Teen Opens Up About Mental Illness," 23ABC News, February 8, 2017. www.turnto23.com/news/local-news/breakingsilence-local-teen-opens-up-about-mental-illness.

Susanna Schrobsdorff, "Teen Depression and Anxiety: Why the Kids Are Not Alright," *Time*, November 7, 2016. http://time.com/4547322/american-teens-anxious-depressed-overwhelmed.

Valerie Strauss, "What Obsessive-Compulsive Disorder Does to a Young Mind When It Grows Unchecked," *Washington Post*, December 11, 2016. www.washingtonpost.com/news/answer-sheet/wp/2016/10/11/what-obsessive-compulsive-disorder-does-to-a-young-mind-when-it-grows-unchecked/?utm_term=.d99207ab5d77.

Index

Picture Credits

Cover: MrPants/iStockphoto.com

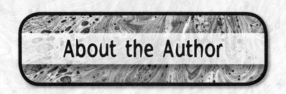

Peggy J. Parks holds a bachelor of science degree from Aquinas College in Grand Rapids, Michigan, where she graduated magna cum laude. An author who has written dozens of educational books on a wide variety of topics for teens and young adults, Parks lives in Muskegon, Michigan, a town she says inspires her writing because of its location on the shores of beautiful Lake Michigan.